THE DRIFT

THE DRIFT

Alan Jenkins

Chatto & Windus
LONDON

Published by Chatto & Windus 2000

2 4 6 8 10 9 7 5 3 1

Copyright © Alan Jenkins 2000

First published in Great Britain in 2000 by
Chatto & Windus
Random House, 20 Vauxhall Bridge Road,
London SW1V 2SA

Random House Australia (Pty) Limited
20 Alfred Street, Milsons Point, Sydney,
New South Wales 2061, Australia

Random House New Zealand Limited
18 Poland Road, Glenfield,
Auckland 10, New Zealand

Random House (Pty) Limited
Endulini, 5A Jubilee Road, Parktown 2193, South Africa

The Random House Group Limited Reg. No. 954009
www.randomhouse.co.uk

A CIP catalogue record for this book
is available from the British Library

ISBN 0 7011 6921 4

Papers used by Random House UK Limited are natural,
recylable products made from wood grown in sustainable forests.
The manufacturing processes conform to the environmental
regulations of the country of origin

Typeset by Deltatype Ltd, Birkenhead, Merseyside
Printed and bound in Great Britain by
Creative Print and Design (Wales), Ebbw Vale

CONTENTS

Chopsticks	1
Inheritance	3
Ancient History	4
Galatea	8
London Nautical	10
Poetry	12
Für Elise	13
Brighton Return	14
Albatross	16
Found Among His Papers	17
Houses	20
Street Life	22
The Short Straw	23
Cloudesley Mansions	33
The Road Less Travelled	34
Pisces	36
Barcelona	37
Diary	39
Crash	40
Für Elise (2)	41
Salt	42
Patience	47
Sketching	48
Evidence	51
Park Life	52
Malaya	53
House-clearing	55
Notes	57
Acknowledgements	58

In Memory of Keith McCulloch, 1954–1996

Night and the fabled dead are near . . .

Horace, Odes I.4, *translated by Louis MacNeice*

CHOPSTICKS

She struggles with her chopsticks, and I watch her slyly
as she mounts a two-pronged attack on a mound
of noodles, or pincer-prods a shrivelled prawn around
its dish of gloop. I watch her as she shyly
sets down the chopsticks and picks up a spoon.
Chicken and cashews, sweet-and-sour pork; no shredded beef –
It's too difficult, what with my teeth –
and special fried rice. Dinner will be over soon,

ten years to the night since he died, and I concentrate
on fashioning from my chopsticks a mast
like the masts on the model clipper ships he built
and rebuilt and rebuilt and rebuilt
hour after hour, night after night, working late
threading cotton through the tiny balsa blocks – a stickler for
   detail –
to make the rigging shipshape on the imagined past
into which, in his little room, he'd set sail . . .

Someone's singing, *So merry Christmas, and a happy New Year*
and I tap out the beat with my chopsticks; *Is everything all right?*
You're very quiet. Everything's fine, mother, let me sip my beer
and remember how we sat with him – ten years to the night –
how we sat with him till it was nearly dawn
and watched him try to breathe,
the white bed between us, and him on it, and grief
no easier now there's a tablecloth, a plate with one sad prawn;

remember how I sat at the piano with my sister
to play our duet – 'Chopsticks' – over and over, *ad nauseam*,
killing time until he came in to pour himself a scotch
and start Christmas day. The clipper ships
still have pride of place in the sitting-room, the museum
where I'll sit for a 'nightcap' among his prints and pipes,
and pour myself another scotch from his decanter, and watch
the late film while my mother dozes and my sister,

I

miles away, plays 'Chopsticks', for all I know;
where I'll sit and think of ten years gone and her two cats
   gone,
gone with the Christmas dinners, my grandmother and great-
   aunt,
with the endless Sunday mornings, Billy Cotton on the radio
and the endless Sunday lunches of roast beef,
gone with half her mind and all her teeth;
she watches me as I place my chopsticks together. *Go on,
finish up that last prawn.* But I can't.

INHERITANCE

Herring-bone and fern, this coat
materialized on the grouse-moor,
on ground my self-made great-grandfather treads
ten years before the First World War;
shotgun-cartridges, tobacco-shreds
and dry-flies in the pocket of his coat,

and the slender hip-flask,
silver in its leather sleeve,
tarnished now from trying to relieve
my grandfather's thirst, take off his fear
of rats and snipers and the feeble cheer
that goes up as they go over. Last-nip flask.

On the way to art-school dances
or a Left Book Club lecture (Spain)
my father glances at his gold-plated watch
and slips the flask, half-full of scotch,
back in the pocket of his coat. At Alamein
it stops a shrapnel-shard as he advances

and he comes home, when the war is ended,
to a place where quiet lives are led
(grandfather, father both long dead,
grouse-moor and money all long gone);
a wife and kids are all he gambles on
but some things, like the fence, are never mended.

And he gives me, not yet twenty,
the flask, that I will later lose,
the coat and watch, that I will wear and use
to seem a man in the world I have not fought for,
worked for, even spared much thought for.
This is my inheritance. It is plenty.

ANCIENT HISTORY

*Kids now don't know anything about history. History is Daddy. And
Daddy is history.* (Joseph Brodsky)

Your leaner, younger face, your leather coat –
but for the raked beret, the darker hair
and thirty years, it could be me,
out with a girl, out to impress,
unmannerly, unthinking. The pubs I took them to . . .
That was the time I learnt about the 'real you',
the weekend life you led aboard your boat,
your evening pub-life, gallant, hail-and-well-met
in the Admiral, the Viceroy or the Empress,
favourite of barmaids, at ease among your peers –
jokes followed jokes, doubles followed beers.
At twenty-five, your gaze is challenging, uncertain, self-aware;
your fist clasps a giant enamel army-issue mug of tea
as if it were a pint of Courage. Dutch courage, maybe.

~

'Dutch courage', you called the stoneware bottle of Bols
you brought back from a business trip and stored
in the rich-smelling dark of the sideboard.
It lasted years. A cut-glass, diminutive glass
or two at Christmas, a sip to reward yourself
for mowing the grass or putting up a shelf.
(I came across a painting by a Dutchman, de Bray,
In Praise of Herring, your other little treat.)
And Holland was the Hook, or else Breda,
home to Paul and Els, survivors of the family
who'd shared with you their cellar, rations, fear . . .
They moved on, artists, conventionally free,
you lost touch. To cover your retreat you joined alcohol's
Dads' Army, dug in for the duration, drank it neat.

Neat in its ranks, my Airfix model air force
endlessly prepared to scramble, my miniature shock troops
overran the house. I hefted your old tin helmet
and charged a pillbox in the garden, or
sniped at the grinning toby-jugs above the pelmet
from my fox-hole in the wrecked back room. My war
was loud, bloodthirsty, and a farce,
Hollywood or Pinewood, war-comic stuff. And yours?
I had no way of knowing, and you never spoke
about the names and faces of your six lost years,
your campaigns, North Africa, Sicily, France;
what made you cry out in the night. Was it choice or chance
that brought you us – me, my sister's pop-groups,
our mother's moans – your disappointing peace?

~

'Peace and quiet' was what you said you wanted
when, demobbed, you married the unhappy girl next door
and settled down to make a living by your pen-
and-ink. Well, that didn't work, though peace
and quiet was what you got, and a Box-Brownie camera
for recording holidays at Pop's west-country place,
and Pop's boat to potter on, until
he and it and everything slid down the pan.
('Pop' was my mother's father, portly, RNVR,
the planter-sailor-schoolmaster of her girlish passion.)
That's all ancient history. You seemed not to hear her pleas
to find a better job, but went on being haunted
by those sunsets on the Hamble, and used your skill
on drawings that were always just behind the fashion.

~

The fashion that year in birthday cards
had changed from the Impressionists
to Japanese prints – the 'Fond regards'
that used to come accompanied by *Mists
at Westminster* or *La Serveuse de bière*
now came with *Cranes* of the Edo period, Rimpa school
or (I still have this one) Naganabo's *Owl
in Moonlight*. I was thinking of you looking lost
among the rows of Hokusai's *Great Wave* and wondering
if I had gone too far beyond your ken –
a student wearing pre-war motley, flowing hair –
for Ryecroft R.A.'s *Tall Ships Racing*, when,
my eye drawn up a shingle beach by cables, runners,
I read 'With love' in *Hauled Boats on a Kentish Coast*.

∼

'Kentish Coast' was on the posters at the station
when we set out for day-trips – Folkestone, Dover, Deal –
our 'summer holidays'. The ferry-horn farted, loud
and clear through salt-rich air; the deckchair-crowd
sat resolutely frowning out to sea,
preserving their McGill-inspired integrity;
rock-pools, weak sunshine, towels stiff with sand,
transistors, thermos-flasks. I shivered as I held your hand
and splashed in the shallows, or watched your powerful crawl
until you stopped and, treading water, slick as a seal,
gazed at the grey horizon, the slopping sprawl
that twenty years before you'd plunged into
from a landing-craft, weighed down by rifle, backpack: you,
who'd thought the icy heave might be your last sensation.

∼

Sensationally alive, weathered, fit and well,
hands in the pockets of your anorak,
in Falmouth, on a slipway – dinghies and a ketch –
you frown against the glare and think of getting back
for a mackerel supper, then the Ship and Bell
where you will stay long after closing-time to sketch
old salts in skippers' caps, and big-bummed girls,
all jeans and yachting sweaters, lips and curls . . .
The snap falls from a book of Bentley's cartoon types –
startled aunts, blonde hostesses, black-tie diplomats –
and I am crying for the innocence, the charm
of this thirties, fifties world, shopping baskets, bowler hats:
your world, yet not – who once, in beret, shorts, two stripes,
frowned at the glare and leant on an Egyptian palm.

GALATEA

The Beaulieu river. River. The Hamble. The yacht *Spray*
pointing up into Southampton Water,
skippered by my grandfather, with a crew of three –

his son-in-law, his grandson and his daughter.
My father and mother and me. Wherever. Wherever.
Leaf-crowded banks, my childhood crouched in the bows

as they dipped and slipped towards the sea, and the river
was lost and found, lost and found, endlessly . . .
I sailed north-north-east in search of their old house

and came to where I'd lived with her. The pier. The shingle-
   shelves
where we lay like sea-creatures on the sea-bed,
blind antennae groping; the click-click in my head

was the sound of pebbles falling over themselves,
the sound of her high heels on the street that day,
of the bubble that welled up in her hot centre,

that rose from the sea-bed, burst and re-formed
under her busy fingers, before she let me enter.
The generator throbbed, tugs and dredgers swarmed

in the harbour. Would I find her, shorter-haired, twice-
   married,
crying as she used to when she lay awake
and listened to that squat colossus, watched it rake

our bedroom with its cyclops eye? No, she is spindrift, carried
on the wind, the voice of one ill wind or another
that blows me and my leaking boat no good –

Whenever you go out, in your little craft of wood,
your little craft of words, it will be me you hear,
it will be me reminding you of how you scorned your mother

and all women who loved you (God knows why),
it will be me reminding you that you will die,
it will be me reminding you of everything you fear.

LONDON NAUTICAL

Thamesis suos ubique feret

The boys at my school always used their fists
in bare-knuckle fights behind the boat-sheds,
smoked and talked about 'bunk-ups' in the bog (or 'heads').
Their taxi-driver dads might as well be Communists,
my dad said, since their strikes had closed the docks.
They came from 'down the Old Kent Road', 'down Vauxhall',
they shouted songs with thrilling words, grabbed their cocks
and mimed tossing off up the changing-room wall . . .
They scared me. I stood to attention, stood at ease
when I was told. I didn't know that I was middle-class
or that 'sailor' meant you took it up the arse.
They told me I spoke posh so I dropped my tees
and aitches, picked up a glottal stop – a case
of learn or die. Of saving half my face.

~

Winter mornings, we chipped ice from the oars
and pulled big whalers round an oil-rainbowed dock.
Upright in the stern, Captain Harding-Raynes
blew thick funnels-full of pipe-smoke,
growled his commands. *Nice weather for chilblains.*
A freezing force-five whipped both shores . . .
Back in the chart-room we pored over azimuths.
We tied one matelot to a chair and hoisted him
with block-and-tackle to the ceiling-pipes;
our marlin-spikes flashed as we spliced wire ropes.
Here are the sails that you will learn to trim.
This is the binnacle, and this the compass.
You will learn to spit and swear and make a rumpus,
you will learn our lovely, nautical, national myths.

~

Two months on the training ship *Winston Churchill*; two
months before the mast. It was a privilege,
I was made to understand, I should be as proud
as my father was. To turn it down would be immoral
(though he didn't say as much) was the Captain's view.
But such was the integrity of our quarrel,
I had so scared myself with *Lord of the Flies* and *Lord
Jim* – the film – that I couldn't give headroom
to that three-master under full sail on the open seas,
to its crew of strangers, and myself on board,
clinging in the topgallant shrouds – *friggin' in the rigging*,
we sang; I retreated to my bedroom
and turned the volume on my little mono up to LOUD
for 'Sunshine of Your Love' and 'Tales of Brave Ulysses'.

～

While my father sat downstairs and read *Lord Jim*
I toiled at mysteries, dead-reckoning, latitude
and longitude; I buffed my shoes for starboard watch,
saluted on parade and earned the two green stripes
my mother sewed on my uniform. I was living out his hopes,
although we both knew I would never go to sea.
I could hear Harding-Raynes grunting in the ward-room,
could hear his *Huumph. What sort of attitude
does he call that?* And he was right, what with Sandra's crotch,
sea-salty, sultry, luxuriant as the Malayas
that rotted Jim, the twitching exquisite who haunted me,
paralysed with fear while drowning extras thrashed the foam.
Coward. In the heads, hand cupped round a Players
No. 6, I knew what longing was. For her. For home.

POETRY

Riverside allotments, avenues of beech and oak,
grass-smells drifting over gardens, bonfire-smoke

in the autumn: the Surrey we had been allotted.
I argued with him, stumped upstairs and plotted

revolution or escape, watched by the eye of Che
who recited Baudelaire's *Les femmes damnées*

from my bedroom wall, and I took up the theme
in wet dream after dream after dream . . .

FÜR ELISE

On her answering machine, Beethoven's *petite phrase*
I heard a hundred times a day when I was eight or nine
and my sister, five years older, practising for her exam.
She took her grades so seriously each night brought a migraine;
sometimes she'd stop and shake with fury after just three bars
if she wasn't perfect. And now I wish that I'd learnt too
(I refused the lessons, the piano was *hers*, like the phone)
since even listening can show me for the fraud I am,
a 'music-lover' who can't read a note, and barely understands
the structure of the simplest piece, like this one – let alone
the later string quartets; or, how unhappiness and pain
are made safe and beautiful, far from what I knew
then, and can't handle now – unsmiling silence, my mother's
    sign
of disappointment; the aching head in shaking hands.

BRIGHTON RETURN

A few days off for some fool conference,
and now you drag your hangover round what remains
of the place you wasted five of your best years in –
getting stoned on grass, going out and getting beers in
and getting up to start again at three
and getting off in bedsits, and not getting AIDS –
recalling last night's 'think tank', and the nonsense
talked by G—, and how everyone seemed sober
except for you. The pale sun of late October
warms the stuccoed crescents, red-brick lanes,
shutters of Refreshment Rooms, boarded-up arcades,

and you remember how it was you found each other
in this past-its-best, out-of-season seaside town:
South London boys both mad to make your mark,
as hungry, fierce and hampered as the shark
in the sea-front aquarium, twitching for the sea.
You shared its rooming houses and its thousand pubs;
to you he was the chosen one, the brother
you'd never had, and you grew inseparable here,
among the smells of salt, wet rot, stale beer,
walking into wind and fine rain that would drown
the words you threw away like twice-smoked stubs.

Now he's dead, you scan the all-absolving waters
as, once, you watched a speck far out, beyond the pier,
grow larger, more like him each time it rose and dipped
(always so far removed, so clenched and clipped)
when he swam back in towards you, waiting: he,
so like and unlike you – why should he have drawn
the short straw? Why should he – a wife, a son, two
    daughters . . .
while you . . . Gull-cries and a sudden rasp
of chains, your own life slipping from your grasp –
at the Mini-Golf you watch a golf-ball disappear
into the gulf below your feet, below the little lawn,

and shiver. Go on, past the wrought-iron terraces
of the prom, the storm-lashed, ocean-liner blocks,
blistered beach-huts, silent funfair, Family World's
deserted paddling-pool – to the place that claimed your girl's
unhappiness and yours: a 'clifftop eyrie' –
a bay window, a patched and paper-peeling double room
where the gas fire sighed all winter at your carelessness,
the kitchen where you stirred hot drinks to nurse
her colds, her aches and pains, her 'curse';
past the wind-battered, sea-blue-painted box
(Lifeguard, First Aid) to the cliff-walk, 'The Coombe',

that sandy, scrubby, gorse-dotted bit of ground
where you got her to agree the thing had died
and she ran off in the rain to cry. Rigging whines
and rattles in the yacht marina where you wrote those lines,
'through wood and weeds, washed up' (alliteratively)
'like bottles, torn shoes and a plastic cup, we walked without
a word, and parted'; a giant claw dug up the drowned,
gouged up the sea-floor gravel, and you'd wake
with plaster in your hair, survivors of an earthquake,
or wet and raw, sea-creatures on a slab – she cried
to see those too. Back now, to the gulls' angry shout,

the littered beach, the breakwaters' ancient callouses;
last light on the grimy swell, the scum-topped surf.
Mast-lines clink in moorings that a salt wind scours.
Remember how you used to stand for hours,
hunched deep in your collar, staring out to sea?
The flag with 'Lifeguard' flaps, a swirling tidal wash
slaps the pier's once pearl-white, rusting palaces;
slate-grey breakers chase the foam-tossed shingle
up the shore. Forty, scalding-eyed and single,
you turn back to the town that was your 'turf'.
What now? Refreshments? First Aid? Hours of tosh?

ALBATROSS

Do you still live in your little boat in the sky?
she asked, who once lay and listened to the wind and rain
lash the beech outside, listened to it creak and strain
like a full-rigged schooner; listened to 'Albatross'
by Fleetwood Mac and played along on air guitar . . .
And I do, I do. Seagulls wheel by my windows
or hang bobbing on their strings just long enough
for me to look into their baby faces (should I wear
a seagull, hung round my neck?); crows flap across
the Westway to their crows'-nest, or gather in the bare
beech-tops, huge X-rayed lungs, to watch me die,
it seems to me, while I smoke and wait for what comes,
or pottering after breakfast, playing 'Albatross', throw them
    crumbs
that the wind takes: crumbs of comfort, not comfort enough.

FOUND AMONG HIS PAPERS

And so, all hope of glory gone for good
Like mist that fades before the sun's first heat,
I turned back to Manaus, to the trade in wood,
The preparation of a ghostly fleet.

A year, two years; and now I had to see
Again, before I died, the teeming port
That held a long-enduring lure for me,
Where, among the boats tied up athwart,

I'd first gazed at the long thin stripe of green,
Immeasurably far, the other side,
And at the swift pirogues that plied between;
Where, assailed by beauty, grinning, brown-eyed,

By sacks of manioc, slab-sided fish,
The reek of spices and the open sewer,
I'd first caught the sickness of the English
And feared both its embodiment and cure.

Companions gone, and all contentment gone,
Desire, the cinder of itself, burnt out
(A taste of ashes where it briefly shone)
And each wide purpose shrivelled to a doubt,

Did I truly think then, in the hour of need,
That I would find once more within my reach
The simple, secret and essential seed –
Kew, Malaya, I, and everybody rich?

Could I have known, the first time I went home,
High priest and agent of the scientist's creed,
That in the hold, in trunks of tropic loam
Grew one man's ruin, and another's greed?

I saw the far-off ground of our devotions,
And grove on grove, and villages un-treed,
I saw the rubber-barons and the oceans
Of white blood those groves would ooze and bleed.

And I saw how we had planted desolation;
How on dark river-faces I would read
The death of hope and of each trading-station,
The rotting wharves, the jetties choked with weed.

I loitered on the quayside, haunted bars,
I let the days fall through my useless hands
Dead as dead matter dumped among the stars,
Sweated through nights in dreams of other lands,

Other lives – my own life a kind of dream:
I woke to what I felt I'd never known,
Voices, names, the black and sluggish stream
All lived by, horizons lush and overblown.

But not me. When I'd drunk my fill of rum
And poured it out again, red-eyed, in tears
And told my snivelling tale of how I'd come
This far, from home to hell, and bent the ears

Of the tenth unlucky trader in a week,
And left behind his disbelieving leer
And stumbled into stifling darkness for a leak,
I'd drag my feet down to the harbour, hear

The quiet slap of water round the piles
And look long at the still, black, wrinkled sheet
Of moonlit estuary – beyond, the isles
Too distant for my searching eyes, too sweet

The clear enchantment that I tried to catch
With sobs and gasps of deep-drawn breath, salt breath.
Back to the oil-lamp and the sputtering match,
I called it death-in-life and life-in-death

See Note 1

HOUSES

My mother's silk kimono hung on her bedroom door
in the house they all moved to after the war –
her favourite brother brought it back for her
saying how, in a flash, the world had grown flat and old.
My father told me how everything began to stir
when she put it on for him, flaring red-blue-gold.

It was frayed, moth-eaten, when it came to the house
I was born in. *Nothing lasts*, my father said,
but he was wrong. There's a picture in my head –
houses bent like trees an instant, waving,
springing back, the walls and windows gone, a town
in one hot gust folding silently and lying down –

that's been there ever since I saw it first. Today
nothing seems so solid any more. *Safe as houses*
they sometimes say, but what's worth saving?
I could have sprayed body-parts but I saw another way.
I listened to the outcry from the trading floor
and found myself on it, palm-out, wanting more.

The fast lane took me off my street, off the terraces;
the inside-track led to club rooms and restaurants
and champagne vaults below the City, level with the sewers,
power-weekends, laughing powder with heiresses
in imitation country houses, and a great new dance,
the world passing from the dreamers to the doers

for the first time in years. But what I saw that day
in St James's Park stayed with me too: trees
as big as houses brought down with casual ease
by a mega-wind, root-systems suddenly in view,
intimate, intricate, centuries-hidden, true –
the works exposed while people looked the other way.

They were changing the colour, or trooping the guard,
a bugle blared, a drum was thumping hard
and everything stood to attention, waiting for when
the Household Cavalry's capes and brass blazed out –
a shit-hot stonking show, an almighty shout,
all the king's horses and all the king's men

lined up to prove to a million camera-shutters
that despite the mad, bearded bastards in the gutters
England was still England, so fucking old,
so fucking right . . . Their house-rules left me cold,
their words, *trust* and *family tradition*.
I'd gone for it. And I'd made the big position:

I was running two houses, a wife, a local girl I'd bought
with a bracelet made from some inexpensive ore.
Then it happened, exactly like it had before:
the city folding flat, prices going through the floor
and by the time the shock-waves had reached Singapore
I'd seen the future, nought after nought after nought.

In a high-octane world you don't just fade away,
you burn out and come down in free-fall – Christ, the faxes,
the boats and hotel rooms, Kuala Lumpur, Mandalay . . .
Her new kimono's like a silk pool on the floor
as I sit and smoke and calculate the unpaid taxes.
I've brought the house down, the papers are holding, this is
    war.

See Note 2

STREET LIFE

I come home at all hours; all hours she receives
her callers, her gentlemen friends, upstairs.
In the street, a car draws up, she breaks into a foolish little
   run.
I know her. Even in the rawest weather, she wears
no tights or stockings, leaves three buttons of her blouse
   undone.
Seeing me, calling, she comes over. We are alike, we share
the same sad, comical fear of being caught
together on our corner, of our long views falling
short, of being caught, of being caught.
Flirting with me, she fiddles with her hair, her shoes,
makes something up when I ask her how she got the bruise
that cascades down her cheek, the purples, reds and blues
of a fruit tart; the colours, almost, of my glans the night
I paid her twenty quid and pushed it up her, dry and tight.

THE SHORT STRAW

You were telling me again how Heinrich Schliemann
had discovered Troy, and George Grote, who was *the* man
in England, was blown out of the water – we were scrambling
  up
the hill above Knossos, you were so far ahead
your voice drifted back to me from the bottom of a well, the
  well
'into which a courtier of Minos might have dipped his cup',

and suddenly I was alone with the vast blue silence
of the sky and the Aegean and the blaze between two islands,
with the green flames of cypresses and the white bull in its
  cave;
there among the other black-eyed, straight-nosed girls who
  stare
for ever into the future from their wall, was Annie's grave
Minoan face, her mouth opening to tell me you were dead . . .

Too late. Too late for us to patch up our quarrel,
for me to award you the palm and you to give me the laurel
as we sit to ouzo and retsina and a huge heaped plate of meat
that is nameless, that you, having set to, name and eat
in a back-street taverna, the owner calling out
Why aren't you eating my liver, and you, *As Prometheus said*

to the vulture; too late to laugh at our falling out
over little cakes and honey in Ammonia Square,
to settle our differences in the garden of the British School
where you showed me Byron's letter and Evans's chair;
too late to recall our laughing fits, the cackle and drool
of the old crone who served us *horta* every night, and our
  dread

of her snaggle-toothed fixed grin, and the shits and squits
that were, you insisted, her revenge – she was one of the
   Furies,
one of the Erinnys, and we had been found by all the juries
of all the gods and heroes, guilty of the crime of contempt;
too late to tell you of the different fate I dreamt
for you: the Eumenides appeared at your deathbed

and they were kind, they treated you kindly, they called off
the white coats and the black suits and finally they hauled off
the great bird that had its beak and talons in your entrails,
so you got up and went home and, since you were forty-one,
the age at which Schliemann gave up the day-job 'and all it
   entails'
and set sail for Asia Minor, you let yourself be led

by your nose for the salt-sown fields, for the smell
of the wine-dark seas off Crete and the meat-smell of
   Heraklion,
the whiff of burning charcoal and the resin-smell of wine
poured from a plump wooden cask, you picked up the thread
and followed it back into the labyrinth, past the steaming pits;
the minotaur had been killed, and you were well, you felt fine.

      ∼

The day I heard, a day like any other, was for you
one of the days that you had left, one of the few.
Annie told me. She thought I might want to write
and I did, I meant to, to make up for years without a word –
but instead I went back to the out-of-season seaside town
that chose us, and it hadn't changed, it hadn't heard:

the terrace-crowded hills that fanned out to meet my train,
the salt wind and the fine insistent rain
had not changed, nor the fairground bulbs that put the *bright*
in Brighton, nor the Grand, the Metropole, the squares
of rust-streaked stuccoed houses, market streets, sea-airs;
and the bookie and the resting actor hadn't heard

of the glamour and the pain of being us, how we'd gone
    down
to rotting B&Bs, the red-brick box that was our birthright,
the library steps that lifted us above our station;
two bookworms who dressed older than our years,
who had no time for the time-pissing politics of our peers,
striking poses over coffee in the common room's mass
    exhalation

of Gitanes-smoke; how you stood your ground
on the 'obvious superiority' of Graves to Pound,
Steely Dan to the Stones, Empson to anyone 'meretricious',
    'trite'
or, worse, 'unmetrical'. When you went back to Loeb and Ee-
sky-lus,
eschewing villanelles for good, I tried not to take it
    personally –
husband-to-be, you had to defend the fortress you had made

(the dinner-things washed up, the breakfast-table laid)
against the armies of the mad, wife-beaters, druggies, drunks;
    against
the fans of Che, the friends of Chile, the iron-fisted, iron-
    gloved
of Czechoslovakia; against my playing part-time anchorite
when I wasn't playing part-time *poète maudit* . . .
Now it's been breached, and the wise moderation that kept
    you tensed

and was so hard-won, looks like the kind of sick joke I once
  loved –
Beckettian, Hitchcockian – I once found so much to my taste
but haven't now the stomach for, and *A stupid waste*
is all I can think, confused, contrite
and queasy as if we'd been on the beer. But it's you who are
  so sick
your stomach's almost gone, on whom time has played this
  trick,

mindless, meaningless; and when I heard you'd said, half
  Waugh,
half Stoic, 'I seem to have drawn the short straw,'
I felt all your bravery and all your fright,
the years dissolved, I was that same night-owl, that same night-
  hawk,
I saw you put a cigarette to pursed, fastidious lips, set down
  the stylus
on 'Katy Lied', or slam outside to walk and walk.

~

As I did, when I heard, I went back down
to walk the beach, to talk it all away, or clear my head –
but I couldn't put my finger on the flaw,
I couldn't see why you should have drawn the short straw
and I should still be here, picking up the thread
and reeling in the years, breathing salt-rich air;

however many times I muttered to myself *It isn't fair*
no one would come to make it all all right.
How could you, who sat up quietly reasoning all night
to make sense of the mess of Maggie's and Joanna's lives,
leave me with these loose ends, unreasonable, a rack of knives
honed by memory, that cut me whenever I go near them?

So many things to ask, though you can't hear them –
How did you shake off the demon-muses that we served
and live well? Did I get more of everything than I deserved,
while you got less? Did we outgrow those boys who stood at
    a slant
to the universe, who drawled *The more things happen to you, the
    more you can't*
tell or remember even what they were – an inseparable, insufferable
    pair?

Now it's pointless, why do I remember how we'd wail, 'I –
I wish I could swim' with Bowie going full-tilt, and dismay
    all-comers
with our paraplegic-robot dance? Remember two long
    summers
of taking papers to the beach and watching with one eye
as the language-students peeled off jeans and T-shirts, and our
    despair
at the sight of beautiful, Parisienne Brigitte, and the way

I fell in love so easily and wanted to be led astray?
Pindar and *Phèdre*, regular metres and irregular verbs?
And 'popping next door' to the pub, and our *confrères*
and *soeurs*, George and Kate and Ian and Nicole, and all the
    beers,
and all of us dancing to 'Dance away the heartache, dance
    away the tears'
and my 'fundamentally irresponsible attitude to herbs'?

Remember the laurel in our tiny yard, and our cat stalking
    there?
Christ, won't you answer me, or look up and frown?
You can't, for fuck's sake, I'm still talking to myself,
talking as I slog through the salt wind and rain
to The Railway Bell, a quick five, then back on the train
where I see you, suddenly, jump up to the bookshelf

and with one of your great asthmatic gulps of breath
take down your precious pre-Socratics, saying *Death
is nothing, dying all; it must not be allowed to scare
old men or girls. In every street and square, behind the rows
of rusting balconies, our lives are being lived by those
who will never know us, or know we lived, and will not care.*

〜

Which leaves me precisely where? In the lurch,
at a loss, in tears in Great Malvern's Priory church
for all the times you diffidently starred,
time out of mind: the times you made a meal
out of making dinner and served up a blistered, charred
and ruined rump of something or other, and intoned, 'Behold,

a burnt offering to the household gods'; the times you told
that joke – once, in a dingy Athens hotel-room with a bottle
of Metaxas and 'the best view of the Acropolis by night'
and we watched it all appear in hazy morning light,
by which time you had conveyed the essence of Aristotle
and the all-important break with Plato; and the times, surreal

but oh-so-real, I took it into my poor head to drown,
my poor drink-maddened head, and I went down
to the shore and flopped into the surf, and you fished me out;
the time I taught you the use of rod and line and reel
and you caught everything in that stream, you even caught a
    trout;
the time on a sweat-and-smoke-filled night train through
    France

you expounded Descartes, in a nicotine-and-coffee trance,
to a carriage-full of soldier-boys ('*Esprit,*'
you said, '*esprit* and *corps* are quite distinct, you see?');
the time you let rip at the top of Devil's Dyke,
Andra moi ennepe . . . to a few sheep and a solitary shrike
and, as you went on, Homer's lines exerted their appeal;

the time you gently but firmly showed the door
to that barking-mad, blood-caked, gate-crashing bore,
or showed a clean pair of heels – though one of them, your
    'Achilles heel',
was thick with bandages – to us, the tribe of Keith,
as we shambled up the hill towards Blackheath
one Sunday lunchtime; the times I discoursed on the void

according to Sartre and Camus, and summoned Proust and
    Freud
as witness to the depth and darkness of our self-deceptions
and called on Swift and Celan, Oedipus and Lear
to speak the unspeakable, the brass tacks of our raw deal;
and you countered with Epicurus, *What is there to fear?*
and insisted that *Call no man happy* must admit exceptions,

that rather than be stymied by the tragic sense of life
we must look to the future, we must find a wife
and let love be our guide and not the words of long-dead
    men;
the times I this, the times you that . . . *Those times*
are gone, and if you now console yourself by making rhymes
I'm glad for you; sorry for the hurts you strive to heal.

                ∼

But I am gone too, and your words can't make me live again.
You made the pilgrimage to the place where we were young –
'South London boys both mad to make our mark,
as hungry, fierce and hampered as the shark
in the sea-front aquarium' – not bad. Isn't this
a bit much, though, so far from the usual vinegar-and-piss,

some might think you were overdoing it? Aren't I a hiccup,
a hiatus in the line of heroes you set out to elegize?
I wasn't famous like some of your other friends,
the scribblers and the chatterers who, when one of them dies,
line up to write the obit. and deliver the memorial address.
I worked hard, loved the life that I was lent and died unsung,

a provincial schoolmaster, far outside the latest trends,
the fads and fashions in the supplements, the Sunday press
such as became your life. I gave up drink and clung
to order, to the middle way, the balanced view;
it was clear to both of us we were on different paths, it's true,
at sixes and sevens, and the harm went unrepaired.

But you must know all things change, and all things stay the same:
that's not the wisdom of the ashram, far-fetched, far-flung
hippy-trippy stuff. Or sophistry. The self I mastered —
prince of the common-room, of the pub when I was plastered —
is clay; I am my loved ones' memories, a name . . .
My genes live on, my mind, in yours and younger heads, as well.

And your spirit, so lofty and hilarious, so highly-strung?
I thought you judged me. I was sure you could pick up
the acrid reek of my pretensions and self-love, the stench
of affectation I gave off whenever I despaired —
those lines I was always quoting, 'Why, this is hell,
nor am I out of it', and more besides, more esoteric, French . . .

I thought you a blind fool for leaving Annie, yes,
and I didn't share your épater les bourgeois taste
in art and literature, your nostalgie de la boue, your fierce
attachment to the weird and arcane, to extremes, to excess;
I didn't trust the charlatans you plunged head-first among,
I didn't think thrash-rock the music of the spheres.

But I absolve you of all that, and abjure you not to waste
whatever time you may have left. Reeling in the years?
Living in the past, I call it. Look ahead, look higher,
lift up your voice a little and give tongue
in your own words, not Leonard Cohen's; tune your lyre,
pick up the thread, the loose ends. That choir . . . .

                     ~

And Bach rings out now that you have gone into the ground
and I am going back to my life, my life that is wrong,
that I cannot put right, and we have gone our ways
again. *In ihm leben, weben und sind wir,*
the words I cannot believe, that you believed, both prayer and
    praise,
praise endlessly; and all of love is in that sound,

it is farewell and greeting, welcome in a quiet house, rest.
Vergnügte Ruh', beliebte Seelenlust, they all join in song
who did their best and are done with it, those ordinary souls,
our fathers and mothers, and Laura's father and Nicole's –
so thin, so elegantly dressed – and all are smiling, they hear
the music that is all about them, each a special guest

and each just like the others. *Heute wirst du mit mir
im Paradies sein* they sing, and for a moment this is true,
truer than the only world I shared with you:
democracy of lecture-halls, of cold damp rooms!
Democracy of dead white males, our pantheon, cold in their
    tombs!
And you are in your grave, and so are Robert Graves

and William Empson, Philip Larkin, Francis Bacon, Sam.
Beckett (as he signed himself that time in my theatre
    programme),
Tim Buckley, Harry Nilsson, Marvin Gaye; they share the
    earth
and the equal sky with emperors, footsloggers, free men, slaves,
with Racine and Callimachus, Velázquez and Vermeer.
Süßer Frieden, stille Ruh' – but I must labour, I must bring to
    birth

this child of grief on memory, and so I think of Bach,
'the most stupendous miracle', his not-a-moment's-doubt
that music was a gift from God; why should we not weep
with sombre joy to hear that huge host sing, *Ach,*
wäre doch mein Abschied hier, mit Freuden sagt' ich, Welt, zu dir:
ich habe genug? I have enough, I ask no more, devout

and calm of heart, of tranquil mind, like Simeon I see
die Freude jenes Lebens schon – the joy of that other life.
There you sit amid the male-voice choir of almighty heaven,
the chorus of the dead, it is February 1727
and Bach conducts you all in this, his first great work of that
    year;
he is forty-two, the age you did not quite come to be,

the age I am now, though I have neither wife
nor child (*Vergnügte Ruh', stille Ruh'*) and you are dead,
my tears are for myself, since death is but a sleep
and a forgetting; you sing, *In deine Hände befehl ich*
meinen Geist, and instead of forgetting there is music,
there is song, *Have mercy on us, Lord, deliver us from fear.*

CLOUDESLEY MANSIONS

(Naked Torso)

I woke in a cloud of garlic-breath, garlic-sweat
and watched through your half-open window
two clouds come together and apart.

You were already awake, and after an hour or so
when I glimpsed you through the half-open bathroom door
your head was in the steamy clouds of Ecuador,

my head had disappeared in the clouds of a cigarette,
the cloudy milk that pooled in a rubber on the floor
answered the clouded glass of water by the bed

and a cloud was forming, for all I know,
on a recent X-ray of my heart,
still palpitating, quick-quick-slow.

THE ROAD LESS TRAVELLED

I've never scaled the heights of Macchu Picchu with a
     backpack
or trekked through India, breakfasting on hunger,
or listened in the African night to the insects' claptrap,
smoked a peace-pipe on Big Sur, or surfed Down Under.

I never featured on the cork board in your kitchen
among the postcards from the friends who'd gone to Goa,
Guatemala, Guam; among the glossy shots of lichen-
and liana-festooned temples, girls who grin *Aloa!*

I never wrote, 'I have walked the sands of Dar-es-Salaam
and seen elephants drink from the great Zambezi';
'Moving on to Bogota'; 'Babar says *Salaam*
from San Francisco'; 'Here in Maui the living's easy'.

(I always sent my greetings from a *caffe*, *camera* or *chambre*
with a view of the Rose Window, Bridge of Sighs,
     Alhambra . . .)

But if I stand on my roof-top in London, West Eleven
with my head in the clouds of Cloudesley Place, North One
I can get it clear: how one day you'll move earth and heaven
to have me here, but I'll have changed tack, I'll be gone

in search of some more fascinating place or person,
I'll have made a fresh start, with no thought, now, of failure,
it won't be my emotions that you play on (or rehearse on),
it won't be my tongue that tastes the coastline of Australia

in the birthmark on your thigh; it won't be me who brings
   you
tea in bed, or a cappuccino with the froth still on it,
or performs my 'Dance to Morning' for you, or sings you
'The Shadow of your Smile', or writes a double sonnet

to you, to your freckled breasts, your sturdy
dancer's legs and neat behind (or, if that's too wordy

for your answering machine, ghazals
to your eyes that are the colour of the clear green water
of Sardinia), or puts on 'El cant dels ocells' by Casals
and holds the phone up to the speaker, or holds your daughter
to the sunrise in a suburban garden with galahs
and kookaburras, holds her up as if I'd caught her
to hear the song of the Catalan birds, and Bala's.

PISCES

How many times, how many times
will I interrupt my sister's morning dreams
with the small spiny perch I yanked out of the Thames,
brought back in a bait-tin half-alive,
left overnight to marinade in its own glair
and dangled in her face that Sunday, 1965?

How many evenings, over a dish
of sea-bass, sole or some other fish,
will I tell of letting go my hold on the steering
in our slender aluminium canoe
when the great bright back of a pirarucu
broke the surface of the Amazon two yards upstream?

How often will I fuss
over heads and fins and tails
for the both of us, only to hear her screams?
How many of its scales
will I bring home and fashion into earrings
that you will never, ever, wear?

BARCELONA

What was I doing here, haunting the dead?
From his studio in a derelict cigarette factory
the windowless windows of the derelict warehouse opposite
were blind eyes overlooking the ochres and umbers
of his palette – I saw his corduroys and scarf,
his slicked-back hair, his head thrown back to laugh
a nineteenth-century, *La Bohème* laugh. But he was gone
and I sniffed stale air for a word I could use,
a word for his life, his art, for the night he went
to be chosen to die by a thing he did not choose,
did not see . . . It was late, I wanted to go to bed
with his beautiful German widow, but she talked me
into submission and downstairs to the *calle*
where someone was shouting and waving a knife
at a woman, his girlfriend, model, wife . . .
Back on the Rambla there was safety in numbers,
or so I thought. I wanted you. It was your scent
I'd caught, wandering by day around the gothic quarter
where you had struggled through a 'difficult' year
on a language-teacher's wage; I'd joined the throng
in the cathedral cloister, stood below its vault
of tattered palms and counted seven fat white geese
that gobble-squabbled under them, for crumbs, for release,
then at my hotel in the little square
I'd sat with chestnut blossom falling in my beer
and imagined it falling in your hair;
when I had to eat, I'd breathed in every tapas bar
the now-familiar amalgam that you are –
the sweet, the garlicky-pungent and the salt –
and remembered you come dripping from the water
for me to frame in the crook of your freckled arm
our cubist village and its single palm,
our spaghetti-western beach, deserted for a shoot-out
at high noon, when sunlight struck it like a gong.
I'd remembered how I 'wore my impatience on my sleeve'.

But what was this drift or shift, like condom-littered sands
along the shore? This searching fingers of left hands
for seals of ownership, and hiding old defeats?
I was heading for the waterfront – God's truth –
to drink in its wind-braced, salt-stiffened air
when the Rambla caught me in its wave and bore me on
to a little, red-lit, low-lit booth
where I watched two strangers – brisk,
methodical, expressionless – ride out their storm;
slap, *slap*, he ploughed her salty furrow, warm
and wet and open wide, he gave no thought to risk
as he poured ambergris into her waiting mouth –
and tugging at myself, so raw and dry,
I wanted to believe, in art that doesn't die,
in whatever lives on in a gothic-baroque-cubist heaven
with sea-nymphs riding dolphins, sea-creatures, shells,
with clouds and putti, far from these semen smells,
blade-and-needle-sharpened, blind-eyed streets.

DIARY

I should not have your read your diary. Maybe,
I thought, you would not have left it open on the floor
if you hadn't wanted me to read those things
you never could have said. But then the words
that spoke so thrillingly about your other lives –
with me not in them, anywhere! – leapt like knives
from your hand, and I knew I'd chosen
my own hurt, and yours. I'd wanted us to be –
not *free bloody birds*, but the galahs with painted wings
on your parasol, heading for the sun; I'd wanted to write
ghazals to your eyes that reminded me of the sea,
not read the endearments you'd entered there, the trite
and tender phrases about him, and not me . . .
But you were rich and strange to me once more,
rich and strange with all the little razor-strands
that cut me when I took the diary in my hands.

CRASH

You'd lost your pearls. You told me as we slowed
to single file past churning lights, an ambulance, the rain
reflecting red off tarmac and the shiny backs
of accident POLICE. Everything turned raw –
from our slog towards a sleety last resort
through laurel-crowded suburbs suffering the weather,
to the box without a sea-view, the over-priced hotel
(its panelled lounge, school-dinners smell
and *Reader's Digests*, its walks for neither health nor sport),
then this, the stove-in metal and approaching chainsaw.
And you had lost your pearls.

They were the snake-dance that we did together,
they were the little globes of light that shone
to light my darkness where they fell, where you fell,
backwards on the duvet, plumply pillowed. They were all
you took with you when you made tracks
to here, your little something for a rainy day,
a present from your mother, part of who you were,
her daughter, far from home – *and what were they to her,*
a single row of Japanese pearls, what were they to her,
the chambermaid who found them? You stopped to make a call
from the next service-area and looked like death
warmed up by neon and we both knew they were gone.

The tail-back cleared, you swung into the fast lane
and put your foot down to the floor and kept it there,
the car held on, held its track towards the white
pearl-strings and necklaces of London, you held on tight,
tight-mouthed the whole way back while I held my breath . . .
I could see you, naked but for your pearls, a cliché
I still tasted, I could remember making you a small
gift of pearls that glittered on your breast, your chin
then melted off. I glimpsed them in the windscreen
as the bright rain hit it and was swiped away.

40

FÜR ELISE (2)

Tu parles joual? From high above the grey St Lawrence,
the early settlers' houses were a stage-set, out of scale.
The fields of Abraham. The field of battle. We'd made peace
abruptly in the hotel lift one night, after three days
of sparring over lunch and dinner, speaking looks
in the special papers and the plenary sessions, unspoken stuff
joking with the late-night crowd in the St Lawrence bar.
The kernel of the hard core, I called her, Elise, young star
of Montreal, Quebec City; I could see through the tough
and witty surface, see into the pale grey eyes and the books
of poems for what she wanted me to see, or so the pale gaze
seemed to tell me; I knew the craving for release
that a single mother like her must . . . I couldn't fail.
Tu vas jouir? Three months of phone calls. Letters. Torrents.

(*Joual*: A form of popular French spoken in Quebec province and
particularly in Montreal. Though attacked as ungrammatical, phoneti-
cally corrupt and full of Anglicisms, it has been adopted by many
Québecois writers since the 1960s.)

SALT

The morning after, the morning of the memorial affair
for Michael V., Michael 'mine's a treble bourbon
and [a line of] coke' Vermuelen, I walked shakily into
   Hangover Square
and a voice in my ear whispered, 'Are you still that suburban
boy who dreamed of taking opium with Baudelaire

or wine with Byron, of setting sail from Greenwich to Durban
with Sir Francis Chichester? Will you never learn –
that some mistakes are final, that the heart gives out,
gives up, that you should expect the unexpected turn
of events that leaves you all at sea, that whoever lives out

of a hip-flask and a coke-spoon has it coming to him, or to
   her?
You've been in the wind and rain of your inner weather
for so long, you've barely noticed what's been going on.
The world has dumbed down, the century is almost gone.
I'd say it was time you got your shit together.

Remember summer evenings when that smell came off the
   reach,
greenish wood at waterline, froth that factories had spilt,
dead gulls, dead fish, tidal leavings, pungent silt –
remember treasure-twitchers on the pram-wheel-littered beach,
the words you cannot outgrow: *trade routes, Trafalgar,*

circumnavigation; do you think the tides will bring a glimpse
of the fabulous, of the man's life, sunk to the hilt
in your place and nation, you might have led if not for your
   vulgar
wish to make it with these middle-men, the pushers, pimps
of literature? I may be smiling as I always was, but look
   twice –

I knew what everyone was worth, I knew your price
and what each of you had or hadn't failed to make
of your enormous luck. Everything I did was its own double-
    take.
Some nights I'd work till dawn to make my Guyville yours
and I was king and you did my bidding and I opened doors.

Who would have thought I might exhaust the vast store of
    me?
(The bottles and the lines lined up. I dispatched them with
    contempt.)
All the signs were there, but none of you ever dreamt . . .'
Later that same day (for I have drawn a veil
of hot tears and old malt and songs that never fail

across the afternoon, and night was falling fast)
I saw a plaque on both the houses I was swaying past –
the one belonged to Francis Chichester,
the other to Frederick Chopin. I whistled a Chopin nocturne
and suddenly I was all business in the stern

of *Gypsy Moth IV*; on board were Brad Leithauser, dressed
in the sailor-suit he wore in *Querelle de Brest*,
and an old salt, made of sterner stuff; but where
were Chichester – Sir Francis – and Frederick Chopin?
Where were they now, when I needed them most?

When I'd mislaid the next bar, and that lighthouse was a lamp-
    post?
And where were Christopher and Edward, *mes copains*?
Suddenly the same voice was serenading me:
'You will never achieve an expression of love for the sea
like the *chansons* of Chausson, or hear what song the sirens

sang to Claude Debussy; you will never find yourself in irons
with Conrad. Your verse bobs like a little yacht
in heavy seas, dismasted, it veers and bobs and weaves
as if it were the *Galatea* at the mercy of great waves,
as if the helmsman were unfit, a soak, a sot

who didn't know his perihelion from his periplum
or periplus, his pabulum from opium or rum.'
When, I thought, when had I been blown off course?
For there they were on my starboard beam,
two white ladies on the rocks, a blessing and a curse.

There came faintly to my ears a snatch
of that old Dylan number, 'You can be in my dream
if I can be in your dream', and I'd picked up a dose, natch,
from a pick-up in the last port of call –
which might have been Portobello or Porthcawl,

it hardly mattered – a market street, a narrow strait
where I used to jib and tack and navigate
between the packing crates, remnants of commercial passion
and the hulks becalmed in a Sargasso of yesterday's news,
yesterday's rotting fruit and veg, their loafing crews

cupping hands round steaming mugs and yawning,
where I would come about and heave to in the early morning,
put in to some safe haven, drink my coffee ration
and remember how I went upstairs with Margery or Kate –
it hardly mattered now that I was drifting, out of drinking
    water,

past a coast of jagged rocks and pines (*O my daughter*)
and it could have been a wharf in Soho or Shad Thames
that loomed out of the fog, pale outstretched hands
groping for the gunwhale, clutching stems
of glasses or belaying pins, pens, brushes, swollen glands,

I heard the gentle slaps of water as it rocked the hull
and the voice of some dead master, mariner,
both one and many, friend and foe, in the cry of a gull
that came through the 'small hushed waves' repeated fresh
   collapse',
I knew the face that bobbed before me in the updraft

and beckoned me towards the cockpit, but when I went aft
the deck had disappeared, I stood in shit-clouded shallows
and the bird flapped and flew around my head: 'Aloes.
A little something for the weekend. Ambre Solaire.
Jojoba. Such were the unguents that you'd apply

to salve each other's arms and legs and backs
when you'd burnt them. *Life's a beach, and then you die* –
Remember that? How mad for the sun you were?
And all the trains in which you made impoverished tracks
through France to the Italian riviera, *mare*

mediterraneo? You were on a pilgrimage, to Rapallo's
boulevards where Pound had strolled, to Sestri
that surprised you with the Via Byron and his old
palazzo on the 'Bay of Silence', and Livorno where
they plucked out Shelley's heart and burned the rest –

'the darkness he embraced was nurse not bride',
that line you both loved . . . Remember the violence
of your last coming together, and what you later wrote,
that stuff about the cyclops in the new marina
and your Galatea, your *sunt lacrimae* note,

all salt and water, half-remembered myth:
'we walked without a word, and parted'? My arse.
Scenes, tears, a year of learning your three Rs –
remorse, regret, recrimination – that's what it took,
and afterwards you put the whole lot in a book

45

and told the world how much you loved her, but it was a
    lie . . .
Half the time you are your own worst enemy
and now you're back to taste her seaweed-and-salt
and ask yourself if it was all your fault
as you've done a thousand times; or do you hope to have
    her sea-anemone

for the price of a double at the Grand? Have you no shame?
Put it behind you, as you have your jottings from
the boudoir of some provincial Don Juan, and refrain
from opening old wounds, scratching at old sores.
These rocks and breakwaters, this pebble beach, this prom

lashed by the English waves, the English rain,
will always call you back – what metaphors
could better anchor you to the permanence of loss?
Love and work, the imperatives I leave you with –
I, your conscience and your albatross –

are all you have. You've grasped you're no more immortal
    than
your friends, than any mother's son, any mortal man;
so cast off your moorings, take the helm
and steer your own course until you can be free,
attached and free. Deep water need not overwhelm

or threaten you. Your end is life. Put out to sea.'

PATIENCE

If I think of my grandmother's house, I think of these:
the black lacquered cabinet of curiosities
that held a Buddha and his temple, intricately carved
in ivory that was yellowing like old teeth, like the keys

when I lifted the lid of the polished, black, upright
piano that no one ever played, that made a soft, blurred,
tuneless noise, half-felt; of the diminishing black herd
of elephants that patiently crossed the mantelpiece

towards the water-hole on the wall to their right,
and how, as they trooped and bellowed, trooped and calved,
all that was left of the real herd after forty years,
they bore witness to the skill of ivory-workers . . .

Nelly the elephant, I sang, aged four, close to tears,
packed her trunk and said goodbye to the circus;
off she went with a trumpety-trump, trump –
trump trump, yelling along to the wireless as I pedalled

my tricycle furiously round the floor
under the eye of the black, beribboned and bemedalled
grandfather clock, between the legs of the green baize
table on which my grandmother laid out cards for patience,

running the gauntlet of frowning vague relations
faster and faster, round and round, one eye on the door
but tied it seemed to the settee, prickly old frump,
the trembling, tintinnabulating nest of trays.

Was it the boldness of her move that drove me on
and the thought of her all alone that made me want to cry?
For forty years I have been trying to say goodbye
but I did not want them to leave me, and I have not gone.

47

SKETCHING

It was September
but it was summer,
a day out of the blue,
so I had ridden miles
along the tidal river,
following my nose,
the smell of mud and diesel,
'coming up from Richmond
on the way to Kew' –
when he stepped from behind
a great horse-chestnut,
split-cane rod in hand,
and said *In vain, in vain*
have I sought you
among the withies and
the sunken, rotted piles
and overhanging willows
on this stretch of towpath
where we used to stand
for hours, where I taught you
the use of rod and spinner
and how to bait a hook,
a sixteen or even smaller size;
in vain have I fetched
fizzy drinks and brought you
sausage rolls, pork pies.
Now have you come
to fish with me again?
Or have you brought my brush,
my paper and my easel?
And what's that mountain-bike?
What happened to the Raleigh racer
I saved for and bought you?
And I could only say, Dad,
you're looking thinner.

Why did you leave your son
when we had all this –
the broken breakwater
on the little muddy reach,
water-lit, white-painted hulls
and the shingle beach
guarded by two gulls?
Before I'd become
part-owner, crew
of the sloop *Galatea*,
Cheverton 1959,
I wish you could see her . . .
And these houses on the river –
Eyot Lodge, Tide View –
they seem now like all I ever
wanted, all I ever knew . . .
Now come on, old lad.
As sure as you, the time come,
left us and your home,
I had to go. As for your mum
I could hardly face her . . .
Think how she suffered mentally
for all she left unsaid,
all I did or left undone.
With that he faded. Once
he seemed to stop, look round
and smiling, gently
as always, wave, that gentle man . . .
And day was fading also when
I turned back home, back
to my hutch, to my den
(it was September
and the days were shorter);
a cold wind sketched
quick hatchings on
the surface where a single swan
took flight from tumbled water

into the last of the sun,
a pike torpedoed, unseen,
unheard, to attack
its meal of fry, and someone
kissed his little daughter,
knowing he would die.

EVIDENCE

They are fading now, the snapshots in envelopes,
postcards I sent her, afterthoughts she kept,
the cards he sent her from his posting in Egypt,
the sleeves of *La Bohème* and the *Hot Club de Paris*,

and whole thick albums of the photographs
he took, on honeymoon, in which she turns and laughs
at the camera, on holidays, that catch her waving
from the gravel drive of that big house with phlox

and rhododendron while my sister points at me;
like the ink in ration books and National Savings,
on deeds and death certificates in the iron box
in the kitchen cupboard, and the *Mails* they lined it with,

brittle-yellow, and the beauties in *Penthouse* and *Jade*
I found among the bunting and the sketching books
in his drawer, pages stuck together where he came;
all are fading, all will fade

until there's nothing left but dust, a memory-myth,
a complex whiff of loneliness and shame,
of developing fluid and old pot-pourri,
old rags, mildewed leather, fishing hooks

that tear me as I leave here, hauling all this on two ropes.

PARK LIFE

The families are all here in long-shadowed sadness
with picnic-littered lawns, duck-ponds and horse-chestnuts
that remind me of childhood and what has not replaced it;
art must have solitude, said Proust, but wanting art I managed
only ruined eyesight, hangovers and sometimes a fit
of rhyming pique. Choice or chance? It hardly matters,
and then only to myself; in a book somewhere the damage
is recorded – I would like to say a broken heart
but that is merely dust-filled which was lust-filled at the start,
those whom I have sent away are well-rewarded
by the thought of the sour taste of the truths I have hoarded
and I have achieved this: a Prozac calm that nothing shatters
when I cast my bread upon the waters, a sadness
that scalds my eyes as the sun dies in a blaze of horse-
    chestnuts.

MALAYA

In Bayswater, where she came to live
to save her mother's life, she forgot Malaya,
the rubber trees, the heat and the verandah,
her amah, and her brother's ayah.

To save her life, she forgot: Malaya
and her mother slowly wasting, fading
in the slow wet heat. Her brother's ayah
saw a white blur on the darkness, saw

their mother slowly wasting, fading
in St Mary's Paddington, attended
by King George V, Queen Mary; a blur, then darkness; saw
her father at the bedside, tight-lipped, sobbing.

In St Mary's Paddington, attended
by the angels and ministers of mercy, her mother
saw her father at the bedside, tight-lipped, sobbing,
though she did not watch. Her mother died –

angels and ministers of mercy, her mother –
when she was ten years too young
to know that as her mother died
half of her father died also.

When she was ten years too young,
too young for fear, for emptiness,
the other half of her father died also,
his heart breaking on the garden path.

Too young for fear, for emptiness
that called to her as she wheeled a pram –
her heart breaking – on the garden path,
she saw the life that started in her baby son,

who called to her as she wheeled his pram,
called to her from his cot. At last
she saw the life that started in her baby son,
the life she'd live, since nothing else was left.

Called to her from my cot, at last
I found myself, after forty years –
the life she'd lived, and nothing else was left –
walking away from her, towards her too.

I found myself, after forty years,
in Bayswater, where I'd come to live;
walking away from her, towards her two
homes, the ice rink, the heat and the verandah.

HOUSE-CLEARING

Her clothes are going into big black plastic sacks
which I tie up, for charity; she no longer needs them,
they are things that have not fitted her for years.
And this *Life* of Cary Grant, these paperbacks
I brought her – *The Penguin Book of Cats, Too Deep For Tears* –
they must go as well, she no longer reads them
and I'd say, judging from the dust they've gathered,
hasn't done in years; nor, though she blah'd and blathered

with the neighbours endlessly about my books,
has she opened *those* since – when? since she was moved to
   tears
by how *unhappy* all my poems made me sound?
For here they are, as dusty as the others, and as useless.
And when did she last refer to *Married Love in Later Years*?
Towards the end they slept in single beds, and looks,
hard looks, were all that passed between them, drowned
in scotch and disappointment. Now she's toothless

and the legs that, as a girl, she was famous for
have started to give her hell, and she must leave her house
which we both call home, as in 'Are you coming home
for Christmas?', and I can't believe her house
holds so much of her: her clothes in cupboards; in her drawer
a sheaf of letters, handwritten, tied with ribbon, and a poem
cut from Patience Strong; on her dressing-table, lavender-water,
scented handkerchiefs, heirlooms of an only daughter.

Who dreamt that I would be here, wrapping up her life,
her fifty years in this one place as daughter, mother, wife,
wrapping up the precious china and cut glass
for sale by auction, tying up loose ends?
That I would find these notes from relatives and friends,
fusty, black-edged, 'With deepest sympathy',
these snaps that show her, a cut above, in her convent-class,
then the woman of the house, house-proud, holding me?

House-proud! The Hoover sucks up a carpet of dust
from the carpet, her sheets and pillow-slips are streaked
and a smell of stale pee hangs about in the hall.
The sideboards and the dinner-service and the toby-jugs, all
that they inherited, accumulated, held in trust
for the family 'overseas', everything that leaked
quiet desperation, wrongness – the home she built:
it must go, and she must go. What's left is guilt.

NOTES

1. 'Found Among His Papers'

Following the invention of vulcanization by Nelson Goodyear in 1839 and the rapid proliferation of uses for rubber in industrial manufacturing, Bolivia, Brazil, Peru and Venezuela, the source of three commercial rubber trees – *Castilla elastica, Hevea brasiliensis* and *Manihot glaziovii* – enjoyed a rubber boom. Richard Spruce, a solitary British botanist and plant collector in Amazonia, presented the Royal Botanic Gardens at Kew with its first herbarium specimens of rubber trees in 1854 and described in *Hooker's Journal of Botany* in 1855 how they were tapped. By the early 1870s the India Office, having commissioned a report on the state of the world's rubber industry, was seeking the opinion of Joseph Hooker, Kew's Director, on the exploitation of India's indigenous rubber tree, *Ficus elastica*, and on whether *Hevea* seeds obtained from Brazil should first be germinated at Kew and the seedlings despatched to India. In 1876, a consignment of Brazilian seeds procured by Sir Henry Alexander Wickham, a British wanderer who had traded in bird plumage in Central America and tried coffee planting in Brazil, was 'smuggled' back to England (Wickham, a flamboyant character, was widely thought to have romanticised the incident) and germinated at Kew. Over the next decade the three important rubber-producing trees of South America were successfully established in British colonial possessions in the East: Ceylon, India, Singapore and, especially, Malaya. Another European rubber boom followed John Dunlop's marketing of the pneumatic tyre in 1888 and the expansion of the car industry, and, by the outbreak of the First World War, rubber production in Malaya and the Dutch East Indies had outstripped that of Brazil. (See Ray Desmond's *Kew: The History of the Royal Botanic Gardens*, 1995.) The speaker of the poem is to be imagined as an agent for a colonial concern, who accompanied one of the Brazilian expeditions – Wickham's, or Robert Cross's – and then returned to the Amazon, 'went native' and disappeared, perhaps died, and in some form of after-life is being punished for his 'enterprise'. Of this aspect of the British rubber trade Desmond comments, 'Leaving aside the legality of the affair, one may ask whether it was an honourable thing to take the natural resources of a country and in so doing deprive it of some commercial advantage.'

2. 'Houses'

Early in 1995, after the Kobe earthquake had precipitated collapse throughout the Far Eastern markets, Nick Leeson, employed by the merchant banking house of Barings (est. 1762) to oversee their securities operations in Singapore, was found to have lost hundreds of millions of pounds of the bank's and its clients' money trading on the 'futures' (and later options) markets – losses he had successfully concealed from his employers for over two years. The bank went bust, and Leeson, after going on the run with his wife, was arrested and sentenced to gaol. During the boom years of the 1980s and again in the 1990s, large numbers of young men and women from conspicuously unprivileged backgrounds made their fortunes on the financial and stock markets of the City of London.

ACKNOWLEDGEMENTS

Thanks are due to the editors of the following publications, in which some of these poems, or different versions of them, first appeared: *Agenda*; the *Guardian*; the *Times Literary Supplement*; *Mind Readings: Writers' Journeys Through Mental States*, edited by Sara Dunn, Blake Morrison and Michèle Roberts; *Time's Tidings: Greeting the 21st Century*, edited by Carol Ann Duffy; and *Oral*, edited by Sarah-Jane Lovett. 'Found Among His Papers' was first published as a Prospero Poets pamphlet (series editor Simon Rae), with linocuts by John Griffiths. The author gratefully acknowledges the assistance of the Lannan Foundation.